Pour le CD audio :

Voix : Lauren et Phil Wharton

Musiques arrangées et orchestrées : Solhal

Chansons enregistrées : par le studio E-magine

www.flammarion-jeunesse.fr
© Flammarion, 2016
Éditions Flammarion – 87, quai Panhard-et-Levassor – 75647 Paris Cedex 13
ISBN : 978-2-0813-7475-1 – N° d'édition : L.01EJDN001209.C003
Dépôt légal : octobre 2016
Imprimé en Asie par APS en octobre 2017
Loi n° 49-956 du 16 juillet 1949 sur les publications destinées à la jeunesse

Sommaire

Old MacDonald Had a Farm 8

Five Little Ducks 10

Mary Had a Little Lamb 12

Baa Baa Black Sheep 14

Humpty Dumpty 16

Polly Put the Kettle on 18

Bring Back (My Bonnie Lies Over the Sea) 20

Grand Old Duke of York 22

Three Blind Mice 24

Pussy Cat 26

Two Little Dicky Birds 28

Jack and Jill 30

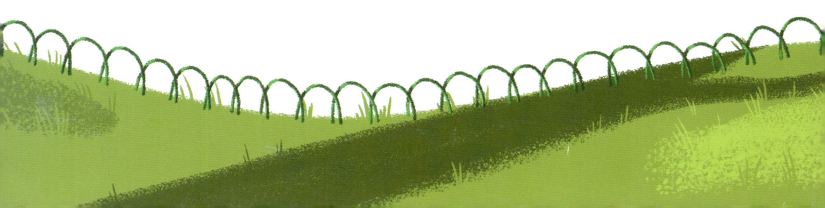

Are You Sleeping Brother John? 32
Oranges and Lemons 34
London Bridge Is Falling Down 36
Hey Diddle Diddle 38
Twinkle Twinkle Little Star 40
One Little Finger 42
Hickory Dickory Dock 44
Rain Rain Go Away 46
Incy Wincy Spider 48
Row Row Row Your Boat 50
1, 2, 3, 4, 5, Once I Caught a Fish Alive 52
The Wheels on the Bus 54
Head, Shoulders, Knees and Toes 56
Little Snowflake 58
Jingle Bells 60

Old MacDonald Had a Farm

Cette célèbre comptine date de 1917 ; le fermier s'appelait alors MacDougal.
Aujourd'hui, toutes ses variantes permettent, sur un air entraînant, de découvrir les animaux de la ferme et leur cri.

Old MacDonald had a farm, Ee-i-ee-i-o,
And on that farm he had a duck, Ee-i-ee-i-o,
With a quack-quack here, and a quack-quack there,
Here a quack, there a quack,
Everywhere a quack-quack;
Old MacDonald had a farm, Ee-i-ee-i-o.

Old MacDonald had a farm, Ee-i-ee-i-o,
And on that farm he had a sheep, Ee-i-ee-i-o,
With a baa-baa here, and a baa-baa there,
Here a baa, there a baa,
Everywhere a baa-baa;
Old MacDonald had a farm, Ee-i-ee-i-o.

Old MacDonald had a farm, Ee-i-ee-i-o,
And on that farm he had a pig, Ee-i-ee-i-o,
With an oink-oink here, and an oink-oink there…

Old MacDonald had a farm, Ee-i-ee-i-o,
And on that farm he had a horse, Ee-i-ee-i-o,
With a neigh-neigh here, and a neigh-neigh there…

Old MacDonald had a farm, Ee-i-ee-i-o,
And on that farm he had a cow, Ee-i-ee-i-o,
With a moo-moo here, and a moo-moo there…

Old MacDonald had a farm, Ee-i-ee-i-o,
And on that farm he had a dog, Ee-i-ee-i-o,
With a bow-wow here, and a bow-wow there…

Five Little Ducks

Utilisée auprès des plus jeunes pour apprendre à compter, on peut mimer la chanson ainsi :
la main droite a 5 doigts écartés ; à « Over the hill and far away », cacher la main derrière le dos.
Mimer la maman de la main gauche, et faire revenir la main droite avec 4 doigts écartés, etc.

Five little ducks
Went out one day
Over the hill and far away
Mother duck said
"Quack, quack, quack, quack."
But only four little ducks came back.

Four little ducks
Went out one day
Over the hill and far away
Mother duck said
"Quack, quack, quack, quack."
But only three little ducks came back.

Three little ducks
Went out one day
Over the hill and far away
Mother duck said
"Quack, quack, quack, quack."
But only two little ducks came back.

Two little ducks
Went out one day
Over the hill and far away
Mother duck said
"Quack, quack, quack, quack."
But only one little duck came back.

One little duck
Went out one day
Over the hill and far away
Mother duck said
"Quack, quack, quack, quack."
But no little duck came back.

Sad mother duck
Went out one day
Over the hill and far away
The sad mother duck said
"Quack, quack, quack."
And all the five little ducks came back.

Mary Had a Little Lamb

*Mary a réellement existé. Au XIXe siècle, aux États-Unis,
cette petite fille amena son agneau à l'école, provoquant le rire de tous ses camarades.*

Mary had a little lamb,
Little lamb, little lamb,
Mary had a little lamb,
Whose fleece was white as snow.

And everywhere that Mary went,
Mary went, Mary went,
And everywhere that Mary went,
The lamb was sure to go.

It followed her to school one day
School one day, school one day,
It followed her to school one day,
Which was against the rules.

It made the children laugh and play,
Laugh and play, laugh and play,
It made the children laugh and play,
To see a lamb at school.

And so the teacher turned it out,
Turned it out, turned it out,
And so the teacher turned it out,
But still it lingered near.

And waited patiently about,
Patiently about, patiently about,
And waited patiently about,
Till Mary did appear.

"Why does the lamb love Mary so?"
Love Mary so? Love Mary so?
"Why does the lamb love Mary so?"
The eager children cry.

"Why, Mary loves the lamb, you know."
The lamb, you know, the lamb, you know,
"Why, Mary loves the lamb, you know",
The teacher did reply.

Baa Baa Black Sheep

Sur un air proche d'Ah ! vous dirai-je, Maman, cette comptine serait une critique de la taxe sur la laine mise en place en Angleterre en 1275.

Baa, baa, black sheep, have you any wool?
Yes sir, yes sir, three bags full!
One for the master,
One for the dame,
And one for the little boy
Who lives down the lane.

Baa, baa, white sheep, have you any wool?
Yes sir, yes sir, three needles full.
One to mend a jumper,
One to mend a frock,
And one for the little girl
With holes in her sock.

Baa, baa, grey sheep, have you any wool?
Yes sir, yes sir, three bags full.
One for the kitten,
One for the cats,
And one for the owner
To knit some woolly hats.

Baa, baa, bare sheep, have you any wool?
No sir, no sir, no bags full.
None for the master,
None for the dame,
And none for the little boy
Who lives down the lane.

Humpty Dumpty

Si l'origine de cette comptine n'est pas claire, le personnage de l'œuf Humpty Dumpty est devenu très populaire dès le XIXe siècle. Il s'invite même dans les films (Le Chat Potté) ou en littérature (Alice : de l'autre côté du miroir).

Humpty Dumpty sat on a wall,
Humpty Dumpty had a great fall;
All the king's horses and all the king's men
Couldn't put Humpty together again.

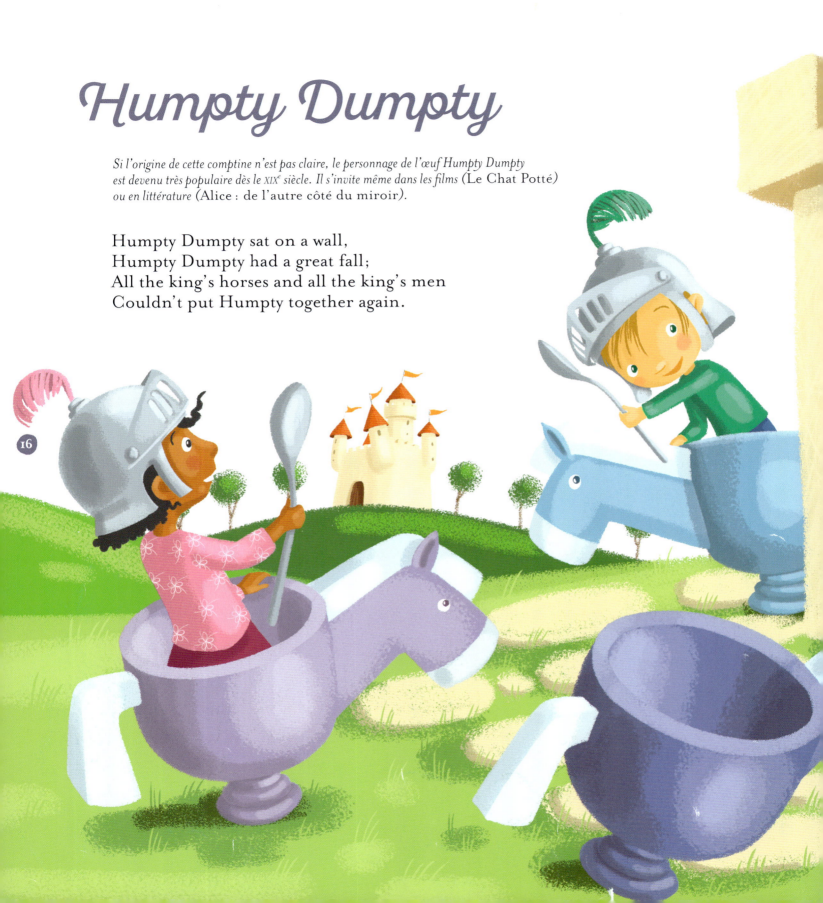

Polly Put the Kettle on

Cette comptine du XVIIIe siècle raconte comment Polly et Sukey faisaient fuir leurs frères en jouant à la dînette avec une bouilloire.

Polly put the kettle on,
Polly put the kettle on,
Polly put the kettle on,
We'll all have tea.

Sukey take it off again,
Sukey take it off again,
Sukey take it off again,
They've all gone away.

Bring Back
(My Bonnie Lies Over the Sea)

Créée au XVIIIe siècle pour réclamer le retour de Charles Stuart sur le trône d'Angleterre, cette chanson est aujourd'hui reprise par les jeunes scouts anglais lors de feux de camp.

My Bonnie lies over the ocean
My Bonnie lies over the sea
My Bonnie lies over the ocean
Oh, bring back my Bonnie to me.

Bring back, bring back
Oh, bring back my Bonnie to me, to me
Bring back, bring back
Oh, bring back my Bonnie to me.

Last night as I lay on my pillow
Last night as I lay on my bed
Last night as I lay on my pillow
I dreamt that my Bonnie was dead.

Bring back, bring back…

Oh, blow the winds o'er the ocean
Oh, blow the winds o'er the sea
Oh, blow the winds o'er the ocean
And bring back my Bonnie to me.

Bring back, bring back…

The winds have blown over the ocean
The winds have blown over the sea
The winds have blown over the ocean
And brought back my Bonnie to me.

Grand Old Duke of York

*Le duc d'York de la chanson serait le prince Frederick,
chef de guerre malheureux lors de la campagne de Flandres en 1794.*

Oh, the grand old Duke of York,
He had ten thousand men;
He marched them up to the top of the hill,
And he marched them down again.

And when they were up, they were up,
And when they were down, they were down,
And when they were only half-way up,
They were neither up nor down.

Three Blind Mice

Cette comptine des 3 souris aveugles peut se chanter en canon.

Three blind mice. Three blind mice.
See how they run. See how they run.
They all ran after the farmer's wife,
Who cut off their tails with a carving knife,
Did you ever see such a sight in your life,
As three blind mice.

Pussy Cat

La reine de la chanson serait Elizabeth Ire, qui fut un jour effrayée par un chat caché sous son trône. Elle accepta sa présence, à condition qu'il chasse les souris du palais.

Pussy cat, pussy cat, where have you been?
I've been to London to see the fair Queen.
Pussy cat, pussy cat, what did you there?
I frightened a little mouse, under her chair.

Two Little Dicky Birds

Cette chanson de 1765 se mime ainsi : un index représente Peter, l'autre Paul. À « Fly away Peter, fly away Paul », on met les mains derrière le dos ; on les ressort à « Come back Peter, comme back Paul ».

Two little dicky birds sitting on a wall,
One named Peter, one named Paul.
Fly away Peter, fly away Paul,
Come back Peter, come back Paul!

Jack and Jill

*Il existe de nombreuses versions de cette comptine du XVIIIe siècle.
Si son origine reste mystérieuse, le papier kraft (« brown paper »)
et le vinaigre (« vinegar ») étaient bien utilisés à cette époque pour soigner les bleus.*

Jack and Jill went up the hill to fetch a pail of water
Jack fell down and broke his crown
And Jill came tumbling after.
Up Jack got, and home did trot
As fast as he could caper
He went to bed and bound his head
With vinegar and brown paper.

Are You Sleeping Brother John?

Cette adaptation anglaise de **Frère Jacques** *peut se chanter en canon et se mimer de la même façon que la version française.*

Are you sleeping, are you sleeping?
Brother John, Brother John?
Morning bells are ringing, morning bells are ringing,
Ding ding dong, ding ding dong.

Oranges and Lemons

Pendant la chanson, les enfants passent chacun leur tour sous le pont formé par les bras des autres enfants ; mais attention à ne pas se faire couper la tête à la fin !

Oranges and lemons,
Say the bells of St. Clement's.

You owe me five farthings,
Say the bells of St. Martin's.

When will you pay me?
Say the bells of Old Bailey.

When I grow rich,
Say the bells of Shoreditch.

When will that be?
Say the bells of Stepney.

I do not know,
Says the great bell of Bow.

Here comes a candle to light you to bed,
And here comes a chopper to chop off your head!

London Bridge Is Falling Down

Cette comptine du XVIIe siècle se joue comme Oranges and Lemons, *mais ici les enfants essaient d'emprisonner les autres entre leurs bras.*

London Bridge is falling down,
Falling down, falling down.
London Bridge is falling down,
My fair lady.

Build it up with wood and clay,
Wood and clay, wood and clay.
Built it up with wood and clay,
My fair lady.

Wood and clay will wash away,
Wash away, wash away…

London Bridge is falling down…

Build it up with bricks and mortar,
Bricks and mortar, bricks and mortar…

Bricks and mortar will not stay,
Will not stay, will not stay…

London Bridge is falling down…

Build it up with iron and steel,
Iron and steel, iron and steel…

Iron and steel will bend and bow,
Bend and bow, bend and bow…

London Bridge is falling down...

Build it up with silver and gold,
Silver and gold, silver and gold...

Silver and gold will be stolen away,
Stolen away, stolen away...

London Bridge is falling down...

Set a man to watch all night,
Watch all night, watch all night...

Suppose the man should fall asleep,
Fall asleep, fall asleep...

London Bridge is falling down...

Give him a pipe to smoke all night,
Smoke all night, smoke all night...

Hey Diddle Diddle

La première trace écrite de cette comptine loufoque date de 1765, mais son origine remonterait jusqu'au XVIe siècle.

Hey diddle diddle,
The cat and the fiddle,
The cow jumped over the moon.
The little dog laughed,
To see such sport,
And the dish ran away with the spoon.

Twinkle Twinkle Little Star

Le poème The star, publié en 1806, a servi de base à cette comptine du soir, chantée sur la mélodie d'Ah ! vous dirai-je, Maman.
Il en existe aujourd'hui de nombreuses versions.

Twinkle, twinkle, little star,
How I wonder what you are!
Up above the world so high,
Like a diamond in the sky.
Twinkle, twinkle, little star,
How I wonder what you are!

Twinkle, twinkle, little star,
How I wonder what you are!
When the blazing sun is gone,
When he nothing shines upon,
Then you show your little light,
Twinkle, twinkle, all the night.

Twinkle, twinkle, little star,
How I wonder what you are!
Then the traveller in the dark,
Thanks you for your tiny spark,
He could not see which way to go,
If you did not twinkle so.

Twinkle, twinkle, little star,
How I wonder what you are!
In the dark blue sky you keep,
And often through my curtains peep,
For you never shut your eye,
Till the sun is in the sky.

Twinkle, twinkle, little star,
How I wonder what you are!
As your bright and tiny spark,
Lights the traveller in the dark,
Though I know not what you are,
Twinkle, twinkle, little star.

Twinkle, twinkle, little star,
How I wonder what you are!
Up above the world so high,
Like a diamond on the sky.
Twinkle, twinkle, little star,
How I wonder what you are!

One Little Finger

Une comptine pour apprendre les parties du corps :
« One little finger », on lève l'index ; « Tap tap tap », on tape l'index levé sur l'autre index ;
« Point your finger up/down », on pointe le haut puis le bas avec l'index levé ;
« Put it on your… », on pose l'index sur la partie du corps.

One little finger, one little finger, one little finger.
Tap tap tap.
Point your finger up.
Point your finger down.
Put it on your head. Head!

One little finger, one little finger, one little finger.
Tap tap tap.
Point your finger up.
Point your finger down.
Put it on your nose. Nose!

One little finger, one little finger, one little finger…
Put it on your chin. Chin!

One little finger, one little finger, one little finger…
Put it on your arm. Arm!

One little finger, one little finger, one little finger…
Put it on your leg. Leg!

One little finger, one little finger, one little finger…
Put it on your foot. Foot!

One little finger, one little finger, one little finger…
Now let's wave goodbye. Goodbye!

Hickory Dickory Dock

Dans cette comptine de 1744, « hickory dickory dock » correspondraient aux chiffres celtes 8, 9 et 10, alors utilisés par les bergers pour compter leurs moutons. Voici une façon rythmée de retenir les chiffres.

A mouse!

Hickory dickory dock. The mouse went up the clock.
The clock struck one. The mouse went down.
Hickory dickory dock.
Tick tock, tick tock, tick tock.
A snake!

Hickory dickory dock. The snake went up the clock.
The clock struck two. The snake went down.
Hickory dickory dock.
Tick tock, tick tock, tick tock.
A squirrel!

Hickory dickory dock. The squirrel went up the clock.
The clock struck three. The squirrel went down.
Hickory dickory dock.
Tick tock, tick tock, tick tock.
A cat!

Hickory dickory dock. The cat went up the clock.
The clock struck four. The cat went down.
Hickory dickory dock.
Tick tock, tick tock, tick tock.
A monkey!

Hickory dickory dock. The monkey went up the clock.
The clock struck five. The monkey went down.
Hickory dickory dock.
Tick tock, tick tock, tick tock.
An elephant… oh no!

Hickory dickory dock. The elephant went up the clock.
Oh no!

Rain Rain Go Away

L'origine de cette comptine serait l'attaque en 1588 de l'Angleterre par la flotte espagnole, repoussée en partie grâce au mauvais temps. Ici, toute la famille rentre en scène.

Rain, rain go away,
Come again another day.
Daddy wants to play.
Rain, rain go away.

Rain, rain go away,
Come again another day.
Mommy wants to play.
Rain, rain go away.

Rain, rain go away,
Come again another day.
Brother wants to play.
Rain, rain go away.

Rain, rain go away,
Come again another day.
Sister wants to play.
Rain, rain go away.

Rain, rain go away,
Come again another day.
Baby wants to play.
Rain, rain go away.

Rain, rain go away,
Come again another day.
Everybody wants to play.
Rain, rain go away.

Incy Wincy Spider

Cette version anglaise de L'Araignée Gypsy s'accompagne d'un jeu de mains qui imite l'araignée en train de monter et descendre.

The Incy Wincy spider
Climbed up the water spout
Down came the rain
And washed the spider out
Out came the sun
And dried up all the rain
So Incy Wincy spider
Climbed up the spout again.

Row Row Row Your Boat

Datant de 1852, cette chanson invite les enfants à s'asseoir l'un en face de l'autre et à faire semblant de ramer en se tenant les mains.

Row, row, row your boat,
Gently down the stream.
Merrily, merrily, merrily, merrily,
Life is but a dream.

Row, row, row your boat,
Gently down the stream.
If you see a crocodile,
Don't forget to scream.

Row, row, row your boat,
Gently down the stream.
Throw your teacher overboard,
And listen to her scream.

Row, row, row your boat,
Gently down the stream.
Ha ha, fooled ya,
I'm a submarine.

Row, row, row your boat,
Gently down the stream.
Merrily, merrily, merrily, merrily,
Life is but a dream.

1, 2, 3, 4, 5, Once I Caught a Fish Alive

Apparue aux alentours de 1765, cette comptine sert depuis souvent de « plouf-plouf » dans les cours d'école.

One, two, three, four, five,
Once I caught a fish alive,
Six, seven, eight, nine, ten,
Then I let it go again.

Why did you let it go?
Because it bit my finger so.
Which finger did it bite?
This little finger on the right.

The Wheels on the Bus

Cette comptine se chante sur la route et peut être continuée à l'infini en décrivant le bruit de chaque objet ou animal croisé.

The wheels on the bus go round and round
Round and round, round and round
The wheels on the bus go round and round
All through the town.

The wipers on the bus go "Swish, swish, swish,
Swish, swish, swish, swish, swish, swish"
The wipers on the bus go "Swish, swish, swish"
All through the town.

The door on the bus goes open and shut…

The horn on the bus goes "Beep, beep, beep"…

The gas on the bus goes "Glug, glug, glug"…

The money on the bus goes "Clink, clink, clink"…

The baby on the bus says, "Wah, wah, wah!"…

The people on the bus say, "Shh, shh, shh"…

The mommy on the bus says, "I love you, I love you, I love you"
The daddy on the bus says, "I love you, too"
All through the town.

Head, Shoulders, Knees and Toes

Cette célèbre comptine date de 1961 et permet d'apprendre les parties du corps en s'amusant à les toucher en rythme.

Head, shoulders, knees and toes
Knees and toes.
Head, shoulders, knees and toes
Knees and toes.
And eyes and ears and mouth and nose.
Head, shoulders, knees and toes,
Knees and toes.

Little Snowflake

En chantant cette comptine, l'enfant imite avec ses mains le flocon qui tombe et se pose sur les différentes parties de son corps.

Snowflake, snowflake, little snowflake.
Falling from the sky.
Snowflake, snowflake, little snowflake
Falling, falling, falling, falling, falling,
Falling, falling, falling, falling
Falling on my head.

Snowflake, snowflake, little snowflake…
Falling on my nose.

Snowflake, snowflake, little snowflake…
Falling in my hand.

Falling on my head.
Falling on my nose.
Falling in my hand.
Snowflake, snowflake, little snowflake.

Jingle Bells

Publiée pour la première fois en 1857, cette comptine a été adaptée en français en 1948 sous le titre **Vive le vent**.

Dashing through the snow
In a one-horse open sleigh
O'er the fields we go
Laughing all the way;
Bells on bobtail ring
Making spirits bright
What fun it is to laugh and sing
A sleighing song tonight!

Jingle bells, jingle bells,
Jingle all the way.
Oh! what fun it is to ride
In a one-horse open sleigh.
Jingle bells, jingle bells,
Jingle all the way.
Oh! what fun it is to ride
In a one-horse open sleigh.

A day or two ago
I thought I'd take a ride
And soon, Miss Fanny Bright
Was seated by my side;
The horse was lean and lank
Misfortune seemed his lot
He got into a drifted bank
And then we got upsot.

Jingle bells, jingle bells…

A day or two ago,
The story I must tell
I went out on the snow,
And on my back I fell;
A gent was riding by
In a one-horse open sleigh,
He laughed as there I sprawling lie,
But quickly drove away.

Jingle bells, jingle bells...

Now the ground is white
Go it while you're young,
Take the girls tonight
And sing this sleighing song;
Just get a bobtailed bay
Two forty as his speed
Hitch him to an open sleigh
And crack! You'll take the lead.

Jingle bells, jingle bells...